the
super bowl
50 Satisfying Soups

Printed in the United States of America
by G&R Publishing Co.

Distributed By:

507 Industrial Street
Waverly, IA 50677

ISBN-13: 978-1-56383-291-8
ISBN-10: 1-56383-291-7
Item # 3611

Table of Contents

Cheesy Chicken Soup

Makes 4 servings

Ingredients

½ lb. skinless boneless chicken
  breast halves

2 T. flour

1 (14 oz.) can chicken broth

2 C. milk

2 C. frozen mixed vegetables

1 C. shredded Cheddar cheese

Directions

Cut the chicken into bite-size pieces. Spray a large saucepan with nonstick cooking spray. Add the chicken to the saucepan and sauté for 5 minutes over medium-high heat, or until the chicken is cooked through. Stir in the flour; heat and stir for an additional minute. Stir in the chicken broth, milk and vegetables; stir until smooth and well combined. Reduce the heat to medium and continue to cook until the soup comes to a boil, stirring often. Remove from heat and stir in Cheddar cheese. Continue to stir until the cheese is completely melted. Ladle the soup into bowls and serve.

Loaded Baked Potato Soup

Makes 4 servings

Ingredients

1 lb. baking potatoes or about 3 C. cubed potatoes

1 (14 oz.) can chicken broth

1 C. milk

3 bacon strips, cooked and crumbled, divided

1 C. shredded Cheddar cheese, divided

2 T. chopped chives, divided

¼ C. sour cream

Directions

Peel and cut the baking potatoes into cubes. Place the cubed potatoes in a large microwave-safe bowl; cover and microwave on high for 5 minutes, stirring after 2½ minutes. Add chicken broth and milk and return to microwave for an additional 10 minutes; stir after 5 minutes. Remove the bowl from the microwave and coarsely mash the potatoes with a potato masher. Set aside 2 tablespoons of the bacon, 2 tablespoons of the Cheddar cheese and 1 tablespoon of the chives for toppings. Add the remaining bacon, cheese and chives to the potato soup; mix well. Ladle the soup into bowls and top each serving with a portion of the reserved bacon, cheese and chives. Add a dollop of sour cream to each bowl.

Tortellini Primavera Soup

Makes 4 to 6 servings

Ingredients

2 (14 oz.) cans chicken broth

1 (9 oz.) pkg. refrigerated
tortellini

2 C. frozen mixed vegetables

1 tsp. dried basil

Dash of hot pepper sauce

2 tsp. cornstarch

¼ C. grated Romano or
Parmesan cheese

Directions

Pour the broth into a large deep skillet or saucepan over high heat; cover and bring to a boil. Stir in the tortellini and reduce the heat to medium-high. Cook uncovered until the pasta is tender, approximately 6 to 8 minutes. Using a slotted spoon, transfer the tortellini to a medium bowl and keep warm. Add the vegetables, basil and hot pepper sauce to the pan with the warm broth. Reduce the heat to medium and simmer for about 3 minutes, or until the vegetables are tender but still crisp. In a small bowl, blend the cornstarch with 1 tablespoon of water. Stir the cornstarch mixture into the soup and cook for about 2 minutes or until the liquid thickens, stirring often. Return the tortellini to the pan and stir. Ladle the soup into bowls and serve.

Barbecued Pork and Bean Soup

Makes 8 servings

Ingredients

2 bacon strips, cut into
    ½" pieces

1 large onion, chopped

1 large clove garlic, chopped

1 T. chili powder

1 tsp. Spanish paprika

2 T. tomato paste

2 T. ketchup

2 T. Dijon mustard

1 (12 oz.) can or bottle beer,
    preferably lager

1 (1½ lb.) fully-cooked smoked,
    boneless pork shoulder

1 (12 oz.) bag coleslaw mix,
    divided

2 (16 oz.) cans white beans or
    4 C. cooked Great Northern
    beans, rinsed and drained

1 chipotle chile, seeded and
    finely chopped

1 tsp. adobo sauce

Directions

In a medium to large soup pot over medium heat, sauté the bacon until the pieces are crisp but not hard. Transfer the bacon to paper towels to drain, reserving the bacon drippings in the pot. Add the onion to the drippings in the pot and sauté until softened, about 5 minutes. Add the garlic and sauté for 1 minute. Stir in the chili powder and paprika, and continue to cook for 30 seconds. Add the tomato paste and sauté for another minute. Mix in the ketchup and mustard, stirring until well blended. Slowly whisk in the beer. Add 8 cups of water and the whole pork shoulder, skimming off any foam on the surface. Reduce the heat to medium, cover the pot and simmer until the pork is tender, about 1 hour. Transfer the pork to a bowl and set aside. Set aside 1 cup of the coleslaw mixture. Add the remaining coleslaw mixture and drained beans to the pot. Simmer uncovered for 10 to 20 minutes. Cut the pork into bite-size chunks, removing any fat, and return to the pot along with any juices from the bowl. Stir in the chile and adobo sauce. Ladle the soup into bowls and garnish each serving with a sprinkling of the reserved coleslaw mix.

Meatball Spinach Soup

Makes 6 to 8 servings

Ingredients

½ lb. lean ground beef

1 C. chopped onion, divided

3 cloves garlic, minced, divided

2 tsp. dried oregano, divided

20 saltine crackers, finely crushed

1 egg, lightly beaten

1 T. vegetable oil

2 (14 oz.) cans beef broth

1 (14.5 oz.) can chopped stewed tomatoes, undrained

1 (10 oz.) pkg. frozen chopped spinach, thawed and drained

Directions

In a medium bowl, combine the ground beef, ¼ cup onion, ⅓ of the garlic and ½ teaspoon oregano. Add the crushed crackers and egg; mix well. Shape the mixture into 1″ meatballs and set aside. Heat the oil in a Dutch oven or large soup pot over medium-high heat. Add the remaining ¾ cup onion and remaining garlic to the oil; sauté for 3 to 5 minutes, or until the onion is tender. Stir in the beef broth, tomatoes with liquid, spinach and remaining oregano. Bring to a boil. Reduce the heat to low and stir in the meatballs. Simmer for 20 to 25 minutes or until the meatballs are cooked through. Ladle the soup into bowls and serve with additional saltine crackers on the side.

Creamy Corn and Turkey Soup

Makes 6 servings

Ingredients

2 T. butter

½ C. chopped onion

1 C. seeded and chopped red bell peppers, divided

4 oz. cream cheese, cubed

1 (14.75 oz.) can cream-style corn

2 C. chicken broth

¾ C. milk

2 C. cooked shredded turkey

Directions

Heat the butter in a Dutch oven or large soup pot over medium-high heat. Add the onion and ½ cup red peppers; sauté until tender, stirring often. Reduce the heat to low and stir in the cream cheese. Continue to heat, stirring constantly, until the cream cheese is melted. Add the corn, chicken broth, milk and shredded turkey. Mix well and cook until the soup is heated through, stirring occasionally. Ladle the soup into bowls and top each serving with a sprinkling of the remaining red peppers.

Souper Tip

To give your soup a thicker consistency, add instant mashed potatoes to the other ingredients in the pot. Or, remove some of the vegetables from the soup, puree in a blender, and then stir them back into the soup.

Italian Sausage Soup

Makes 6 servings

Ingredients

1 lb. Italian sausage

1 clove garlic, minced

2 (14 oz.) cans beef broth

1 (14.5 oz.) can Italian-style stewed tomatoes, undrained

1 C. sliced carrots

¼ tsp. salt

¼ tsp. pepper

2 small zucchini, cubed

1 (14.5 oz.) can Great Northern beans, undrained

2 C. fresh spinach, packed, rinsed and torn

Directions

In a Dutch oven or large soup pot over medium-high heat, brown the Italian sausage and garlic. Once the sausage is browned, stir in the beef broth, stewed tomatoes with liquid, carrots, salt and pepper. Reduce the heat to medium, cover and simmer for 15 minutes. Stir in the zucchini and beans with liquid. Cover and simmer for an additional 15 minutes, or until the zucchini is tender. Remove the pot from the heat and stir in the fresh spinach. Replace the lid and let the spinach steam for about 5 minutes. Ladle the soup into bowls and serve.

Vegetable Beef Soup

Makes 10 servings

Ingredients

1 (3 lb.) beef chuck roast

½ C. quick-cooking barley

1 bay leaf

2 T. vegetable oil

3 medium carrots, chopped

3 stalks celery, chopped

1 large onion, chopped

1 (16 oz.) pkg. frozen mixed
   vegetables

4 cubes beef bouillon

1 T. sugar

¼ tsp. pepper

1 (28 oz.) can chopped stewed
   tomatoes, undrained

Salt and pepper

Directions

Trim the fat from the beef roast. Cook the roast with ½ cup water in a slow cooker for 4 to 5 hours on the high setting. Add the barley and bay leaf for the last hour of cooking time. Remove the roast from the slow cooker and cut into bite-size pieces. Return the beef pieces to the slow cooker, but turn off the heat; set aside. Discard the bay leaf. Heat the vegetable oil in a large soup pot over medium-high heat. Add the carrots, celery, onion and frozen mixed vegetables to the pot; sauté until tender. Stir in 4 cups of water, beef bouillon cubes, sugar, ¼ teaspoon pepper and stewed tomatoes with liquid. Stir in the beef, barley and broth from the slow cooker. Bring the soup to a boil, reduce the heat to medium and simmer for 10 to 20 minutes. Season with salt and additional pepper to taste. Ladle the soup into bowls and serve.

The Best Ham and Potato Soup

Makes 8 servings

Ingredients

3½ C. peeled and diced
   potatoes

⅓ C. diced celery

⅓ C. finely chopped onion

¾ C. cooked diced ham

2 T. chicken bouillon granules

¼ tsp. salt

½ tsp. white pepper

5 T. butter

5 T. flour

2 C. milk

Directions

In a large soup pot over medium-high heat, combine the potatoes, celery, onion, ham and 3¼ cups water. Bring to a boil, then reduce the heat to medium. Cook until the potatoes are tender, about 10 to 15 minutes. Stir in the chicken bouillon, salt and pepper. Melt the butter in a separate saucepan over medium-low heat. Whisk in the flour and cook for about 1 minute, stirring constantly, until the mixture is thick. Slowly stir in the milk, whisking constantly to prevent lumps. Continue to stir until the liquid is thick, about 4 to 5 minutes. Stir the milk mixture into the pot and continue to cook until the soup is heated through. Ladle the soup into bowls and serve.

White Bean Chicken Chili

Makes 9 servings

Ingredients

2 T. vegetable oil

1 medium onion, chopped

2 cloves garlic, minced

1 (14 oz.) can chicken broth

1 (18.75 oz.) can tomatillos, drained and chopped

1 (16 oz.) can diced tomatoes, undrained

1 (7 oz.) can diced green chilies, drained

½ tsp. dried oregano

½ tsp. ground coriander

¼ tsp. ground cumin

2 ears fresh corn

1 lb. cooked, diced chicken

1 (15 oz.) can white beans, drained

Salt and pepper

1 lime, sliced

Directions

Heat the vegetable oil in a large soup pot over medium-high heat. Add the onion and garlic; sauté until tender. Stir in the chicken broth, tomatillos, tomatoes with liquid, chilies, oregano, coriander and cumin. Bring to a boil, then reduce heat to medium and simmer for 10 minutes. Cut the corn from the cob. Add the corn, chicken and beans; simmer for 5 minutes. Season with salt and pepper to taste. Ladle the soup into bowls and garnish each serving with a slice of lime. Other appropriate garnishes include: avocado slices, sour cream, shredded cheese and crushed tortilla chips.

Roasted Chicken Noodle Soup

Makes 8 servings

Ingredients

2 tsp. olive oil

1 C. chopped onion

1 C. chopped carrots

1 C. chopped celery

1 clove garlic, minced

¼ C. flour

½ tsp. dried oregano

¼ tsp. dried thyme

¼ tsp. poultry seasoning

6 C. chicken broth

4 C. peeled diced potatoes, uncooked

1 tsp. salt

2 C. roasted diced chicken breast

2 C. uncooked yolk-free wide noodles

1 C. evaporated milk

Directions

Heat the olive oil in a Dutch oven or large soup pot over medium-high heat. Add the onion, carrots, celery and garlic; sauté for 5 minutes or until the vegetables are tender. Stir in the flour, oregano, thyme and poultry seasoning; mix well and cook for 1 minute. Gradually stir in the chicken broth, potatoes and salt; bring to a boil. Reduce the heat to medium, cover and simmer for 15 to 20 minutes, or until the potatoes are tender. Stir in the chicken and noodles; simmer for 10 additional minutes, or until the noodles are tender. Reduce the heat to low and stir in the evaporated milk. Be careful not to let the soup boil after the milk has been added. Ladle the soup into bowls and serve.

Wild Rice Soup
with Bacon

Makes 4 servings

Ingredients

½ C. uncooked wild rice

3 smoked bacon strips, cut
into ½" pieces

½ C. chopped onion

½ C. chopped celery

½ C. chopped carrots

5 C. chicken broth

1 C. whipping cream

Salt and pepper

Directions

Rinse the wild rice three times under hot running tap water. Fry the bacon pieces in a large soup pot or deep skillet over medium-high heat. Remove the bacon to paper towels to drain and keep warm. Leave about 2 tablespoons of the bacon drippings in the pot. Add the onion, celery, carrots and rice to the pot and cook until the vegetables are tender. Stir in the broth and bring to a boil. Reduce the heat to medium and stir in the cream, salt and pepper. Return the bacon to the pot, cover and simmer for 45 minutes to 1 hour. Ladle the soup into bowls and serve.

Souper Tip

If your soup is too salty, simply place a raw potato
in the soup and simmer for about 15 minutes.
The potato will absorb extra salt.

Smoked Sausage, Bean and Barley Soup

Makes 6 servings

Ingredients

1 (10 oz.) pkg. smoked sausage

1 (15.5 oz.) can Great Northern beans, rinsed and drained

1 (14.5 oz.) can chopped stewed tomatoes, undrained

1 medium onion, chopped

2 stalks celery, sliced

½ C. quick-cooking barley

2 tsp. Worcestershire sauce

½ tsp. dried basil

Dash of hot pepper sauce

Directions

Cut the sausage into ¼"-thick slices. Place the sausage slices into a Dutch oven or large soup pot over medium-high heat. Add the beans, stewed tomatoes with liquid, onion, celery, barley, Worcestershire sauce and basil to the pot. Continue to heat until the soup boils, stirring often. Reduce heat to medium-low, cover and simmer for 15 minutes, or until the vegetables are tender. Season to taste with a dash of hot pepper sauce; mix well. Ladle the soup into bowls and serve.

Taco Soup

Makes 8 servings

Ingredients

1 lb. ground beef

1 large onion, chopped

3 (15.5 oz.) cans Mexican-style chili beans, undrained

1 (15.5 oz.) can whole kernel corn, undrained

1 (15 oz.) can tomato sauce

1 (14.5 oz.) can diced tomatoes, undrained

1 (4.5 oz.) can chopped green chiles, drained

1 (1.25 oz.) env. taco seasoning mix

1 (1 oz.) env. ranch dressing mix

Directions

Brown the ground beef and onion in a Dutch oven or large soup pot over medium-high heat, stirring until the meat crumbles. Drain the fat, keeping the beef and onions in the pot. Stir in the beans with liquid, corn with liquid, tomato sauce, tomatoes with liquid, green chiles, taco seasoning mix, ranch dressing mix and 1½ cups water. Bring the soup to a boil. Reduce the heat to medium and simmer, uncovered, for 15 minutes, stirring occasionally. Ladle the soup into bowls and garnish each serving with a few corn chips. Other appropriate garnishes include: shredded lettuce, chopped tomato, sour cream and shredded Cheddar cheese.

Chinese Vegetable Soup with Pork Meatballs

Makes 4 servings

Ingredients

4 C. chicken broth

¾ C. chopped green onions, divided

2 star anise

1 (3") piece fresh gingerroot, sliced

½ lb. lean ground pork

1 clove garlic, crushed

1½ tsp. minced fresh gingerroot

2 tsp. dry sherry

2 tsp. soy sauce

1 tsp. cornstarch

½ tsp. sugar

½ tsp. salt

Pinch of cayenne pepper

1 T. vegetable oil

2 plum tomatoes, skinned, seeded and diced

8 oz. snow peas, strings removed

Directions

In a large soup pot over medium-high heat, combine the chicken broth, ¼ cup chopped green onions, star anise and gingerroot slices. Bring to a boil, then reduce the heat to low, cover and simmer for 20 minutes. Meanwhile, in a medium bowl, combine the ground pork, garlic, 1½ teaspoons minced gingerroot, sherry, soy sauce, cornstarch, sugar, salt and cayenne pepper; mix by hand until well blended. Shape the mixture into ½″ meatballs and set aside. Heat the vegetable oil in a medium saucepan over medium heat. Add ¼ cup of the remaining green onions; sauté until softened, about 3 minutes. Add the tomatoes and sauté for 1 minute. Meanwhile, strain and discard the green onions, star anise and gingerroot slices from the chicken broth mixture. Stir the tomato mixture into the pot with the broth. Add the snow peas and meatballs to the broth. Continue to cook for 2 minutes after the meatballs rise to the surface, about 6 minutes total. Ladle the soup into bowls and garnish each serving with a sprinkling of the remaining green onions.

Cauliflower and Five Cheese Chowder

Makes 6 servings

Ingredients

3 T. unsalted butter

1 medium red onion, chopped

4 C. chicken broth

1 C. dry white wine

2 T. chopped fresh parsley

3 C. small cauliflower florets

¾ C. milk

1 C. heavy cream, divided

½ C. grated Parmesan cheese

½ C. grated Romano cheese or other sheep's milk cheese

½ C. shredded Gouda cheese

½ C. shredded fontina cheese

¼ C. crumbled Gorgonzola or other blue cheese

1 egg yolk

¼ tsp. ground nutmeg

Salt and white pepper

1 C. combined red and yellow pear or grape tomatoes

2 T. fresh chopped chives

Directions

Melt the butter in a Dutch oven or large soup pot over medium-high heat. Add the onion and sauté until softened, about 7 minutes. Stir in the chicken broth, wine and parsley; bring to a boil. Add the cauliflower, reduce the heat to medium and simmer until tender, about 5 to 7 minutes. Transfer 1 cup of the cauliflower and some of the liquid from the pot to a blender; puree. Add the puree back to the pot and stir in the milk and ¾ cup cream. Add the Parmesan, Romano, Gouda, fontina and Gorgonzola cheeses. Continue to heat, stirring often, until the cheeses are completely melted. In a small bowl, combine the remaining ¼ cup cream, egg yolk and nutmeg. Add a ladleful of hot soup, beating until well blended, then whisk the yolk mixture back into the chowder, being careful not to let the chowder simmer or boil. Season with salt and white pepper to taste. Stir in the tomatoes and cook until they are heated through. Ladle the chowder into bowls and garnish each serving with a sprinkling of chives.

Corn and Cheddar Chowder

Makes 6 servings

Ingredients

3 T. unsalted butter

1 medium onion, chopped

1 large potato, peeled
  and diced

1 bay leaf

½ tsp. cumin

¼ tsp. dried sage

3 T. flour

2 C. chicken broth

1½ C. milk

1½ C. frozen corn kernels

2 T. chopped fresh parsley

2 T. chopped fresh chives

¼ C. dry white wine

2 C. shredded Cheddar cheese

Salt and pepper

Directions

Melt the butter in a Dutch oven or large soup pot over medium-high heat. Add the onion, potato, bay leaf, cumin and sage; sauté for 5 minutes or until the onion is tender. Add the flour, stirring to coat the potato and onion. Stir in the chicken broth and milk; bring to a boil, whisking constantly until smooth. Reduce the heat and simmer for 30 minutes, uncovered, until the potato is tender, stirring often. Mix in the corn, parsley, chives and wine; continue to heat for 5 minutes. Remove the bay leaf and add the Cheddar cheese, stirring until melted. Season with salt and pepper to taste. Ladle the chowder into bowls and serve.

Souper Tip

Most soups, with the exception of fish soups, develop better flavor over time. Always provide enough time to prepare a flavorful soup instead of rushing through the process.

New England Clam Chowder

Makes 4 servings

Ingredients

3 smoked bacon strips

1 medium onion, chopped

2 (6 oz.) cans minced clams

1 (11 oz.) can clam juice

2 medium red potatoes, diced

¾ C. frozen corn kernels

1½ C. milk, preferably 2%

2 tsp. Worcestershire sauce

¾ tsp. dried savory

Salt and pepper

Directions

Fry the bacon in a Dutch oven or large soup pot over medium heat for about 5 minutes. Transfer the bacon to paper towels to drain; crumble and set aside. Add the onion to the bacon drippings in the pot and sauté until tender, about 3 minutes. Drain the clams over the pot through a fine-mesh sieve so the liquid drains into the pot and the clams are reserved. Set aside the clams. Add the clam juice and potatoes to the pot; continue to heat until the potatoes are tender, about 15 to 20 minutes. Transfer half of the chowder mixture to a blender; puree. Return the pureed mixture to the pot. Stir in the corn, milk, Worcestershire sauce, savory and reserved clams. Reduce the heat to low and continue to cook until the chowder is heated through, being careful not to simmer or boil. Season with salt and pepper to taste. Ladle the chowder into bowls and add a sprinkling of crumbled bacon to each serving.

Brie, Carrot and Mushroom Bisque

Makes 8 servings

Ingredients

1½ lbs. Brie cheese

4 T. unsalted butter, divided

1 (8 oz.) pkg. sliced cremini or shiitake mushrooms

1 large leek, cut into ¼" thick rounds

1 (8 oz.) pkg. baby carrots, cut into ¼" thick rounds

3 T. flour

2 C. half n' half, warmed

4 C. chicken broth

2 T. dry sherry

½ tsp. pepper

Garlic-flavored croutons

Directions

Trim and discard the rind from the Brie. Cut the cheese into 1″ chunks and set aside. Melt 1 tablespoon butter in a large soup pot over medium-high heat. Add the mushrooms and sauté for about 5 minutes or until tender. Transfer the sautéed mushrooms to a bowl. Use a paper towel to wipe out the pot. Add the remaining 3 tablespoons butter to the pot. Add the leek and carrots; sauté until tender, about 5 minutes. Stir in the flour, then gradually whisk in the half n' half until smooth. Bring the bisque to a boil for 1 minute, whisking constantly. Add the chicken broth and heat until almost boiling, then add the Brie. Reduce the heat to medium and stir with a wooden spoon until the cheese is completely melted. Add the sherry and pepper; mix well. Stir in the mushrooms and any liquid from the bowl; simmer for 10 minutes. Ladle the bisque into bowls and top each serving with a few croutons.

Simple Lobster Bisque

Makes 4 servings

Ingredients

1 T. butter
¼ C. chopped onion
1½ C. milk
1 (8 oz.) pkg. cream cheese,
  cubed

1½ C. cooked chopped
  lobster meat
¼ tsp. salt
2 T. dry sherry

Directions

Melt the butter in a medium soup pot over medium heat. Add the onion and sauté until tender. Slowly stir in the milk and cream cheese. Continue to heat, stirring occasionally, until the cheese is completely melted. Mix in the lobster, salt and sherry. Continue to cook until heated through. Ladle the bisque into bowls and serve.

For a lower-fat version, use Neufchâtel cheese in place of the cream cheese.

Souper Tip

Freeze the liquids drained from canned mushrooms or other vegetables for later use in soups to add excellent flavor.

Shrimp Bisque

Makes 5 servings

Ingredients

1 T. butter

½ C. sliced celery

1 (8 oz.) pkg. cream cheese, cubed

1 C. milk

½ lb. Velveeta processed cheese, cubed

1 (6 oz.) pkg. small frozen cooked shrimp, thawed and drained

⅓ C. dry white wine

¼ tsp. dried dillweed

Directions

Melt the butter in a medium saucepan over medium heat. Add the celery; sauté until tender. Reduce the heat to low and add the cream cheese and milk, stirring until the cheese is completely melted. Add the Velveeta, shrimp and wine. Continue to heat, stirring often, until the Velveeta is completely melted and the bisque is heated through. Ladle the bisque into bowls and add a sprinkling of dillweed to each serving.

For a lower-fat version, use Neufchâtel cheese in place of the cream cheese. In addition, use Velveeta made with 2% milk, a reduced-fat pasteurized prepared cheese product.

Black-Eyed Pea Gumbo

Makes 8 servings

Ingredients

1 T. olive oil

1 medium onion, chopped

1 medium green bell pepper,
seeded and chopped

5 stalks celery, chopped

2 C. chicken broth

1 C. uncooked brown rice

4 (15 oz.) cans black-eyed
peas, undrained

1 (10 oz.) can diced tomatoes
with green chiles, undrained

1 (14.5 oz.) can diced
tomatoes, undrained

2 cloves garlic, minced

Directions

Heat the olive oil in a large saucepan or soup pot over medium heat. Add the onion, bell pepper and celery; sauté until tender. Add the chicken broth, brown rice, black-eyed peas with liquid, and both kinds of diced tomatoes with liquid. Mix in the garlic and bring the soup to a boil. Reduce the heat to low and simmer uncovered for 45 minutes, or until the rice is tender. If the soup is too thick, stir in a little water. Ladle the gumbo into bowls and serve.

Souper Tip

Ever wonder how much soup to make?
If the soup is not intended as the main course, count on one quart of soup per six adults. If the soup will be a main dish, plan for one quart to serve two to three adults.

Louisiana Gumbo

Makes 20 servings

Ingredients

4 lbs. medium shrimp, unpeeled

½ C. vegetable oil

½ C. flour

1 C. chicken broth

1 (3 lb.) whole chicken

2 large onions, chopped

5 stalks celery, chopped

1 green bell pepper, seeded and chopped

5 large tomatoes, seeded and chopped

4 cloves garlic, minced

2 bay leaves

1 T. salt

2 T. Old Bay seasoning

1 T. ground cayenne pepper

3 (6 oz.) cans crab meat, drained

1 lb. andouille sausage, diced

2 T. filé powder

Directions

Peel and devein the shrimp. Place the removed shells and tails in a very large soup pot and cover with 8 cups water. Set aside the shrimp meat in a bowl and refrigerate until ready to use. Bring the water in the pot to a simmer over medium-low heat until the liquid is reduced by half. Strain out the shells and tails; transfer the shrimp broth to a bowl and set aside. Add the oil to the pot over medium-high heat. Mix in the flour, cooking and stirring with a long handled spoon until the flour is dark brown. Slowly stir in the chicken broth and 1 cup water. Place the whole chicken in the pot. Add the onions, celery, bell pepper, tomatoes, garlic, bay leaves, salt, Old Bay seasoning and cayenne pepper. Bring to a boil and simmer for 1½ hours, or until the chicken is cooked through. Remove the chicken from the pot and set aside until cool enough to handle. Cut the chicken into bite-size pieces, removing any skin and bones. Return the chicken meat to the pot and stir in the reserved shrimp broth, shrimp meat, crab meat and sausage. Add the filé powder and stir, making sure to mix all the way to the bottom of the pot. When the gumbo returns to a boil, remove the pot from the heat. Continue to stir for 1 minute. Discard the bay leaves. Ladle the gumbo into bowls and serve.

Minestrone

Makes 8 servings

Ingredients

¼ C. Italian dressing

1 medium onion, chopped

1 stalk celery, chopped

1 medium carrot, chopped

1 (14.5 oz.) can diced
tomatoes, undrained

1 (19 oz.) can red kidney
beans, drained and rinsed

2 (14 oz.) cans vegetable broth

1 tsp. Italian seasoning

1½ C. uncooked small
shell pasta

½ C. grated Parmesan cheese

Directions

Heat the Italian dressing in a large saucepan or soup pot over medium-high heat. Add the onion, celery and carrot; sauté for 2 minutes, or until the vegetables are tender but still crisp. Add the tomatoes with liquid, kidney beans, vegetable broth, 2 cups water and Italian seasoning. Reduce the heat to medium and simmer for 1 hour. Stir in the uncooked pasta and heat for an additional 10 to 12 minutes or until the pasta is tender. Ladle the soup into bowls and garnish each serving with a sprinkling of Parmesan cheese.

Easy Tuscan Soup

Makes 4 servings

Ingredients

2 T. olive oil

1 medium carrot, sliced

1 medium onion, chopped

1 stalk celery, chopped

2 cloves garlic, minced

1 (15 oz.) can Great Northern beans, drained and rinsed

1 (15 oz.) can black beans, drained and rinsed

1 (14 oz.) can chicken or vegetable broth

½ tsp. dried thyme

Salt and pepper

¼ C. grated Parmesan or Romano cheese

Directions

Heat the oil in a Dutch oven or large soup pot over medium-high heat. Add the carrot, onion, celery and garlic; sauté for 4 to 5 minutes, or until the onions are tender. Stir in the Great Northern beans, black beans, broth and thyme. Bring to a boil, then reduce the heat to medium and simmer for 10 minutes, or until heated through. Season with salt and pepper to taste. Ladle the soup into bowls and garnish each serving with a sprinkling of Parmesan cheese.

Broccoli Dijon Soup

Makes 8 servings

Ingredients

5 C. chicken broth

(10 oz.) pkgs. frozen chopped
  broccoli

¼ C. butter

¼ C. flour

¼ C. Dijon mustard

2 C. half n' half

⅛ tsp. salt

⅛ tsp. pepper

Directions

In a large saucepan or soup pot over high heat, bring the chicken broth and broccoli to a boil. Reduce the heat to low and simmer for 5 minutes, or until the broccoli is tender. Transfer the broth and broccoli to a blender or food processor, working in batches, and process until smooth; set aside. Melt the butter in the same saucepan over medium-high heat. Add the flour and heat for 3 minutes, stirring constantly. Return the blended broccoli mixture to the saucepan and stir in the mustard, mixing well. Continue to cook until the mixture begins to boil and thicken, stirring occasionally. Stir in the half n' half, salt and pepper, mixing well. Continue to cook until the soup is heated through. Ladle the soup into bowls and serve.

Spinach Cheese Soup

Makes 4 servings

Ingredients

1 T. butter

¼ C. chopped onion

2 C. milk

½ lb. Velveeta processed
cheese, cubed

1 (10 oz.) pkg. frozen chopped
spinach, cooked and drained

⅛ tsp. ground nutmeg

Dash of pepper

Directions

Melt the butter in a large saucepan or soup pot over medium heat. Add the onion and sauté until tender. Stir in the milk, Velveeta, spinach, nutmeg and pepper. Reduce the heat to low and cook until the cheese is completely melted and the soup is heated through, stirring occasionally. Ladle the soup into bowls and serve.

For a lower-fat version, use fat-free milk. In addition, use Velveeta made with 2% milk, a reduced-fat pasteurized prepared cheese product.

For a variation, substitute frozen chopped broccoli for the spinach.

French Onion Soup

Makes 2 servings

Ingredients

¼ C. butter

5 medium onions, cut into
   ¼" thick slices

2 bay leaves

2 T. flour

1 C. dry red wine

2 C. beef broth

1 C. chicken broth

2 sprigs fresh rosemary

Salt and pepper

2 baguette slices, toasted

¼ C. shredded fresh Swiss,
   Parmesan or Asiago cheese

Directions

Melt the butter in a Dutch oven or large soup pot over medium-high heat. Add the onion slices and bay leaves. Cover the pot and cook for 15 minutes. Reduce the heat to medium and continue to cook until the onions are deep brown, about 1 to 1½ hours, stirring occasionally. Add a little water, as necessary, to keep the onions from drying out. Sprinkle the flour over the onions and stir; continue to heat for 1 minute. Stir in the wine and cook until the wine has almost been completely reduced. Add the beef broth, chicken broth and rosemary sprigs. Allow the soup to simmer until the liquid has reduced by a quarter. Remove and discard the bay leaves and rosemary sprigs. Season the soup with salt and pepper to taste. To serve, ladle the warm soup into oven-safe bowls and float one baguette slice on the soup in each bowl; sprinkle with the shredded Swiss, Parmesan or Asiago cheese. Heat the bowls under an oven broiler until the cheese has melted.

Seven-Onion Soup

Makes 6 servings

Ingredients

¼ C. unsalted butter

4 shallots, thinly sliced

3 green onions, cut into
   ¼" pieces

2 large leeks, rinsed and cut
   into thin rings

1 large sweet onion, chopped

1 medium red onion, chopped

1 C. mixed red and white
   pearl onions, peeled

1 large carrot, peeled and
   chopped into ½" pieces

1 stalk celery, chopped into
   ½" pieces

1 T. sugar

1 tsp. sea salt

¼ tsp. pepper

6 C. chicken, beef or vegetable
   broth

1 large egg

½ C. olive oil

3 T. fresh lemon juice

Salt and pepper

2 T. dry sherry

¼ C. chopped fresh chives

2 T. chopped fresh parsley

Directions

Melt the butter in a large saucepan over medium-high heat. Add the shallots, green onions, leeks, sweet onion, red onion, pearl onions, carrot and celery; sauté until the vegetables soften, about 5 minutes. Reduce the heat to low and cover the vegetables with a sheet of waxed paper. Cover the pan with the lid and let the vegetables sweat for 10 minutes. Remove the lid and discard the waxed paper. Stir in the sugar, sea salt and ¼ teaspoon pepper; continue to sauté until the vegetables are lightly glazed, stirring often. Stir in the broth and bring the soup to a boil. Reduce the heat to low and simmer, partially covered, for 10 minutes. Meanwhile, in a food processor, blend the egg. While the processor is running, add the oil, pouring in a thin steady stream. Continue to process while adding the lemon juice and ½ cup of the hot soup. Season the blended sauce with salt and pepper to taste. Stir the sherry into the soup in pan and remove from the heat. Add the blended sauce to the soup and stir in the chives and parsley. Continue to cook until heated through, being careful not to let the soup boil. Ladle the soup into bowls and serve.

Tomato Harvest Soup

Makes 4 servings

Ingredients

¼ C. butter

1 C. chopped onion

3 lbs. fresh tomatoes, peeled,
  seeded and chopped

2 T. tomato paste

1 T. sugar

1 tsp. salt

1 tsp. dried basil

½ tsp. dried thyme

¼ tsp. pepper

¼ C. flour

4 C. chicken broth, divided

1 C. heavy cream

Directions

Melt the butter in a large saucepan or soup pot over medium heat. Add the onion and sauté until tender, about 5 minutes. Stir in the tomatoes, tomato paste, sugar, salt, basil, thyme and pepper. Simmer for 10 minutes, stirring occasionally. In a small bowl, combine the flour and ¾ cup chicken broth; mix into a paste. Add the flour mixture and remaining broth to the saucepan. Bring to a boil for 2 minutes, stirring constantly. Reduce the heat to low, cover and simmer for 30 minutes, or until the tomatoes are tender. Remove the saucepan from the heat. Stir in the heavy cream. Immediately ladle the soup into bowls and serve.

Tomato Black Bean Soup

Makes 4 servings

Ingredients

½ C. sun-dried tomato
salad dressing

1 medium yellow onion,
chopped

2 cloves garlic, minced

1 (15 oz.) can black beans,
drained and rinsed

1 (14.5 oz.) can diced
tomatoes, undrained

½ C. quick-cooking barley

1 tsp. dried basil

½ tsp. pepper

1 medium green bell pepper,
seeded and chopped

Directions

Heat the dressing in a large saucepan or soup pot over medium heat. Add the onion and garlic and sauté for 5 minutes, or until the onion is tender. Stir in 4 cups water, black beans, tomatoes with liquid, barley, basil and pepper. Mix well and bring the soup to a boil. Reduce the heat to medium-low and let simmer for 15 minutes, stirring occasionally. Remove the saucepan from the heat. Stir in the bell pepper, cover and let stand for 5 minutes. Ladle the soup into bowls and serve.

Souper Tip

Many soups, especially vegetable soups, are improved in flavor by the addition of a spoonful of shredded cheese, which should be sprinkled over the soup at the time of serving. Crackers, croutons, chopped chives, and sometimes sour cream, also add to the flavor of many soups. These should be spooned onto the surface of the soup just prior to serving.

Cuban Black Bean Soup

Makes 8 servings

Ingredients

2 T. vegetable oil
1 medium onion, chopped
4 cloves garlic, minced
1 T. ground cumin
1 (14 oz.) can chicken broth, divided

3 (16 oz.) cans black beans, undrained, divided
1 (16 oz.) jar thick and chunky salsa
½ C. sour cream

Directions

Heat the vegetable oil in a large saucepan or soup pot over medium heat. Add the onion, garlic and cumin; sauté for 3 minutes. In a blender, combine half of the chicken broth and 1 can of the black beans with liquid; process on high until pureed. Add the pureed mixture to the saucepan. In the blender, blend the remaining chicken broth with another can of the black beans with liquid. Add this mixture to the saucepan. Stir the remaining can of black beans and salsa into the saucepan. Mix well and bring to a boil over medium-high heat. Reduce the heat to low and simmer for 15 minutes, stirring occasionally. Ladle the soup into bowls and place about 1 tablespoon sour cream over each serving.

Sweet Potato Soup

Makes 6 servings

Ingredients

2 bacon strips, cut into
 ¼" pieces

2 stalks celery, cut into ¼" slices

2 medium red onions, diced

1 Golden Delicious apple,
 peeled, cored and cut into
 ½" pieces

2 T. flour

4 C. chicken, beef or vegetable
 broth, divided

3 medium sweet potatoes,
 peeled and cut into ½" pieces

2 C. half n' half

Salt and pepper

½ to 1 C. sour cream or
 plain yogurt

Chopped fresh chives

Directions

In a large saucepan or soup pot over medium-high heat, fry the bacon pieces until crisp but not too hard. Transfer the bacon to paper towels to drain, reserving 2 tablespoons bacon drippings in the saucepan. Add the celery, onions and apple to the saucepan; sauté for about 5 minutes, or until the vegetables and apple pieces have softened. Add the flour and heat, stirring constantly, until well blended. Gradually stir in half of the broth and bring to a boil for 1 minute, stirring constantly. Add the remaining broth and sweet potatoes; return to a boil. Cover and let simmer for about 25 minutes, or until the sweet potatoes are tender but not falling apart. Stir in the half n' half. Continue to cook until heated through, then season with salt and pepper to taste. Ladle the soup into bowls and garnish each serving with a dollop of sour cream, a sprinkling of chives and some of the bacon pieces.

Butternut Squash Soup

Makes 6 servings

Ingredients

*1 (2½ to 3 lb.) butternut
  squash*

¼ C. unsalted butter

1 T. olive oil

*2 medium onions, finely
  chopped*

*8 thin slices peeled fresh
  gingerroot, each about
  2" long*

8 C. milk, divided

1 tsp. sea salt

White pepper to taste

*Chopped fresh mint leaves,
  optional*

Directions

Preheat the oven to 400°. Line a baking sheet with aluminum foil and grease the foil with nonstick cooking spray. Cut the squash in half lengthwise, then scrape out and discard the seeds. Place the halves, cut side down, on the foil. Bake for 50 minutes, or until the squash is tender. The squash is done when a sharp knife or skewer can be inserted easily into the flesh. Remove the squash from the oven and set aside until cool enough to handle. Peel the skin from the squash and dice the flesh. Melt the butter and olive oil in a large saucepan or soup pot over medium-low heat. Add the onions and sauté until softened but not browned, about 10 minutes. Stir in the diced squash and gingerroot slices; sauté for 5 minutes. Reduce the heat to low and stir in 3 cups milk; bring to a simmer. Remove the pot from the heat and transfer the soup to a blender or food processor, working in batches; process until smooth. Return the puree to the pot and stir in the remaining 5 cups milk. Continue to simmer until the soup thickens. The soup should be thick enough to coat the back of a spoon. Season with sea salt and white pepper to taste. Ladle the soup into bowls and garnish each serving with a few chopped mint leaves, if desired.

Chicken Fiesta Soup

Makes 4 servings

Ingredients

¼ C. Italian dressing

¾ lb. skinless boneless chicken breasts, cut into bite-size pieces

1 medium onion, chopped

1 C. chopped stewed tomatoes, undrained

1 (14 oz.) can chicken broth

1 (8.5 oz.) can peas and diced carrots, drained

1 tsp. chili powder

½ C. shredded Mexican-style cheese

Crushed tortilla chips

Sour cream

Directions

Heat the Italian dressing in a large saucepan or soup pot over medium-high heat. Add the chicken and onion; sauté for 5 minutes. Stir in the tomatoes with liquid, chicken broth, peas and carrots, and 1½ cups water. Season with the chili powder and mix well. Bring to a boil. Reduce the heat to medium and simmer for 8 minutes or until the chicken is cooked through and the onions are tender. Preheat the oven broiler. Ladle the soup into four oven-safe bowls and sprinkle 2 tablespoons of the shredded cheese over each serving. Place the bowls 6″ below the broiler for 1 to 2 minutes, or until the cheese is melted. Garnish each serving with a few crushed tortilla chips and a dollop of sour cream.

Turkey and Tofu Miso Soup

Makes 6 servings

Ingredients

12 dried shiitake mushrooms

½ lb. turkey cutlets, cut into strips ¼" wide and 1½" long

½ C. yellow miso

¾ C. snow peas, stems and strings removed

1 lb. firm tofu, cut into strips ¼" wide and 1½" long

Chopped fresh chives

Directions

In a microwave, bring 3 cups of water to a boil in a glass bowl or measuring cup. Add the mushrooms to the boiling water and let soak at least 20 minutes or overnight. Squeeze the liquid from the mushrooms into the bowl and place the mushrooms on a cutting board. Tear off the stems and cut the caps into slivers. Pour the mushroom liquid through a fine-hole sieve into a large saucepan or soup pot over medium-high heat. Add 3 cups cold water and bring to a boil. Stir in the turkey and simmer until the turkey is cooked through, about 6 minutes. In a small bowl, combine the miso and ½ cup of the hot soup; set aside. Bring the remaining soup to a boil. Add the mushrooms and snow peas; simmer for 3 minutes. Add the tofu and heat through. Stir the miso mixture into the soup and continue to heat until the soup is almost boiling. Ladle the soup into bowls and garnish each serving with a sprinkling of chives.

Curried Carrot Soup

Makes 6 servings

Ingredients

1 T. olive oil

1 medium onion, chopped

1 stalk celery, chopped

1 clove garlic, chopped

*2 lbs. unpeeled carrots, cut
into ½" thick rounds*

1 T. curry powder

1 tsp. ground ginger

5 C. chicken broth

*1 C. light coconut milk
or plain yogurt*

Salt and pepper

Directions

Heat the olive oil in a large saucepan or soup pot over medium heat. Add the onion, celery and garlic; sauté until tender, about 5 minutes. Add the carrots and mix well. Stir in the curry powder and ginger. Cook, stirring constantly, for 30 seconds. Stir in the broth and bring to a boil over high heat. Reduce the heat to medium-low and simmer, partially covered, for 30 minutes, or until the carrots are very tender. Transfer the soup to a blender, working in batches, and process until smooth. Return the pureed soup to the pot. Stir in the coconut milk and reduce the heat to low. Continue to heat, but be careful not to let the soup simmer. Season with salt and pepper to taste. Ladle the soup into bowls and serve.

For a less creamy soup, the coconut milk or yogurt can be omitted.

Thai Peanut Chicken Soup

Makes 6 servings

Ingredients

2 T. peanut or vegetable oil

6 large cloves garlic, crushed

3 to 4 Thai chiles, seeded and minced

3 kaffir lime leaves, stem and main vein removed, minced

1 (4") piece fresh lemongrass, thinly sliced

2 shallots, minced

4 C. chicken broth

2 T. fresh lime juice

¼ C. creamy peanut butter

1 (14 oz.) can unsweetened coconut milk, divided

1½ lbs. chicken cutlets, cut into ½" by 1" strips

6 T. Thai or Vietnamese fish sauce

2 T. chopped fresh basil

2 T. chopped fresh cilantro

3 C. prepared jasmine rice

Directions

Heat the oil in a large saucepan or soup pot over medium heat. Add the garlic, chiles, lime leaves, lemongrass and shallots; sauté until the ingredients are very fragrant, about 5 minutes. Stir in the chicken broth and lime juice; bring to a gentle simmer. In a small bowl, blend together the peanut butter and 2 tablespoons coconut milk. Whisk the peanut butter mixture into the soup until well blended. Add the remaining coconut milk and chicken. Return to a gentle simmer until the chicken is cooked through, about 2 minutes. Mix in the fish sauce, basil and cilantro. Place about ½ cup cooked rice in each bowl and ladle the soup over the rice. Serve immediately.

Reuben Soup

Makes 6 servings

Ingredients

2 T. butter

½ C. chopped onion

½ C. sliced celery

1 C. chicken broth

1 C. beef broth

½ tsp. baking soda

2 T. cornstarch

¾ C. sauerkraut, rinsed
and drained

2 C. half n' half

2 C. cooked chopped
corned beef

1 C. shredded Swiss cheese

Salt and pepper

Rye bread croutons

Directions

Melt the butter in a large saucepan or soup pot over medium-high heat. Add the onion and celery; sauté until tender, about 5 minutes. Add the chicken broth, beef broth and baking soda. In a small bowl, combine the cornstarch and 2 tablespoons water; mix well and add to the saucepan. Bring the soup to a boil for 2 minutes, stirring occasionally. Reduce the heat to medium-low and stir in the sauerkraut, half n' half and corned beef; simmer for 15 minutes. Stir in the Swiss cheese and heat until melted. Season with salt and pepper to taste. Ladle the soup into bowls and garnish each serving with a few rye bread croutons.

Souper Tip

Soup can be frozen in freezer-safe zippered plastic bags.
Fill the bags with soup and close tightly. Lay the bags
flat in the freezer. Once the soup is frozen, the bags can
stand on end to help conserve freezer space,
or several bags can be stacked on top of each other.

Lemon Chicken
and Asparagus Soup

Makes 4 servings

Ingredients

2 whole skinless bone-in
    chicken breasts

2 stalks celery, quartered

1 medium onion, quartered

½ tsp. salt

¼ tsp. white pepper

1½ lbs. asparagus

1 C. baby carrots, cut into
    thin rounds

4 egg yolks

1 C. heavy cream

1 T. fresh lemon juice

2 T. chopped fresh parsley

Directions

In a large saucepan or soup pot over medium-high heat, combine 4 cups of water, whole chicken breasts, celery, onion, salt and white pepper. Bring to a boil, reduce the heat to low and simmer until the chicken is almost cooked through, about 20 minutes. Remove from heat and let the chicken cool in the broth, about 30 minutes. Transfer the chicken to a bowl to cool completely, then remove the meat from the bones and cut into thin strips; set aside. Strain the broth through a fine-hole sieve into a clean saucepan. Peel the asparagus, starting 2″ from the tips. Cut the asparagus into 2″ lengths, separating the tips from the stalk pieces. Transfer 2 cups of broth to a medium saucepan and bring to a boil. Prepare a bowl of ice water. Add the asparagus tips and carrots to the broth and boil for 5 minutes. Drain the broth through a fine-hole sieve back into the larger pot. Plunge the asparagus tips and carrots into the ice water; set aside. Transfer another 2 cups of broth to the smaller saucepan and bring to a boil. Add the peeled asparagus pieces and cook until tender. Transfer this mixture to a blender; process until pureed. Return the puree to the larger pot and bring to a boil. Add the chicken, asparagus tips and carrots; reduce heat to medium-low. In a bowl, whisk together egg yolks, cream and ½ cup hot soup. Whisk the cream mixture back into the soup, but do not let simmer or boil. Stir in the lemon juice and parsley. Ladle the soup into bowls and serve.

Shrimp and Feta Soup

Makes 4 servings

Ingredients

1 T. butter

2 T. olive oil

1 medium onion, chopped

2 cloves garlic, minced

5 roma tomatoes, peeled
and chopped

1 (8 oz.) bottle clam juice

1 C. dry white wine

¾ tsp. dried oregano

Pinch of salt

½ tsp. pepper

4 oz. crumbled feta cheese

1 lb. medium shrimp, peeled
and deveined

¼ C. chopped fresh parsley

Directions

Melt the butter in a large soup pot over medium heat. Add the olive oil and heat for 1 minute. Stir in the onion and garlic; sauté until tender. Mix in the tomatoes, clam juice and wine. Stir in the oregano, salt and pepper. Bring the ingredients to a low simmer for 10 minutes. Transfer the soup to a blender, working in batches, and puree until smooth. Return the pureed soup to the pot and stir in the feta cheese. Continue to heat, stirring occasionally, for 10 minutes. Stir the shrimp into the soup and heat for 3 minutes, or until the shrimp turn opaque. Ladle the soup into bowls and garnish each serving with a sprinkling of chopped parsley.

Chilled Cream
of Vegetable Soup

Makes 6 servings

Ingredients

3 sprigs fresh parsley

1 bay leaf

½ tsp. dried thyme

2 whole cloves

1 small clove garlic, crushed

1 C. chopped celery leaves

*1 medium carrot, peeled
and diced*

*1 small green bell pepper,
seeded and diced*

*1 C. finely chopped spinach
leaves*

1 large onion, chopped

4 C. vegetable broth

¼ C. uncooked rice

2 egg yolks

2 C. half n' half

Salt and pepper

Minced fresh chives or parsley

*2 medium tomatoes, peeled,
seeded and chopped*

Directions

Tie the parsley sprigs, bay leaf, thyme, cloves and garlic into a square of cheesecloth to make an herb bundle. In a Dutch oven or large soup pot over medium-high heat, combine the herb bundle, celery leaves, carrot, bell pepper, spinach leaves, onion, vegetable broth and rice; bring to a boil. Reduce the heat to medium and bring to a simmer, partially covered, stirring occasionally. Simmer for about 30 minutes, or until the rice is tender. Remove the pot from the heat and discard the herb bundle. In a blender or food processor, puree the soup until smooth, working in batches. Return the pureed soup to the pot. In a small bowl, whisk together the egg yolks and ½ cup of the hot soup. Return the egg mixture to the soup pot and mix well, but do not let simmer or boil. Stir in the half n' half, salt and pepper; cook until heated through. Remove from heat and let cool completely. Chill the soup in the refrigerator for 1 hour. To serve, whisk the soup vigorously and ladle into chilled bowls. Garnish each serving with chopped chives or parsley and a few tablespoons chopped tomatoes.

Classic Beef Stew

Makes 6 servings

Ingredients

4 large carrots, chopped

2 potatoes, peeled and cubed

1 C. sliced fresh mushrooms

1 large onion, chopped

3 stalks celery, chopped

3 lbs. cubed stew meat

1 (1 oz.) env. dry onion
soup mix

1 (10.75 oz.) can golden
mushroom soup

Directions

Place the carrots, potatoes, mushrooms, onion and celery in a 5-to 6-quart slow cooker. Spread the stew meat over the vegetables. In a medium bowl, combine the dry onion soup mix and golden mushroom soup. Add 1¾ cups water and mix well. Pour the soup mix over the ingredients in the slow cooker. Add additional water until the liquid comes just to the bottom of the meat. Cover the slow cooker and cook on high for 6 hours or on low for at least 9 hours, adding more water as necessary. If you prefer a longer cooking time, the meat, soup and water can be cooked on low for up to 24 hours, adding the vegetables during the last 4 to 8 hours. Ladle the soup into bowls and serve.

Chicken Soup with Dumplings

Makes 8 servings

Ingredients

4 skinless boneless chicken
  breast halves

2 T. butter

2 (10.75 oz.) cans cream of
  chicken soup

1 medium onion, finely diced

2 (10 oz.) pkgs. refrigerated
  biscuit dough, torn into
  pieces

Directions

Cut the chicken into ½″ pieces. Place the chicken, butter, cream of chicken soup and onion in a 3- to 6-quart slow cooker. Fill the slow cooker with enough water to cover the ingredients. Cover the slow cooker and cook on high for 5 to 6 hours. About 30 minutes before serving, place the torn biscuits over the soup in the slow cooker. Cover and continue to cook on the high setting until the biscuit dough is cooked through. Ladle the soup and dumplings into bowls and serve.

Corn Chowder

Makes 8 servings

Ingredients

2½ C. milk

1 (14.75 oz.) can cream-style corn

1 (10.75 oz.) can cream of mushroom soup

1¾ C. frozen corn kernels

1 C. frozen shredded hash browns

1 C. cooked cubed ham

1 large onion, chopped

2 T. butter

2 tsp. dried parsley

Salt and pepper

Directions

Place the milk, cream-style corn and cream of mushroom soup in a 3- to 6-quart slow cooker; mix well. Add the corn kernels, hash browns, ham, onion, butter and parsley. Cover the slow cooker and cook on low for 6 hours. Before serving, season with salt and pepper to taste. Ladle the soup into bowls and serve.

Souper Tip

It can take up to 24 hours for a large stockpot of hot soup to cool in the refrigerator. To properly cool soup in the refrigerator, transfer the soup to several shallow containers, making sure the soup is no more than 2" deep. Place the containers in the refrigerator loosely covered. Cover completely when the soup has cooled.

Sweet Chili

Makes 6 servings

Ingredients

½ C. ketchup

¼ C. molasses

1 tsp. dry mustard

1 (16 oz.) can baked beans
with pork

1 tsp. salt

½ tsp. pepper

4 bacon strips, chopped

1 large green bell pepper,
seeded and chopped

1½ lbs. ground beef

1 tsp. chili powder

Directions

Combine the ketchup, molasses, dry mustard, baked beans, salt and pepper in a 3- to 6-quart slow cooker; mix well. In a large skillet over medium heat, cook the bacon and bell pepper for 5 to 7 minutes, or until the bacon is crisp but not hard. Drain the grease from the skillet and add the cooked bacon and bell pepper to the slow cooker. In the same skillet over medium heat, brown the ground beef. Drain the grease from the cooked ground beef. Add the beef and chili powder to the slow cooker; mix well. Cover the slow cooker and cook on high for at least 1 hour or on low for 3 hours. Ladle the chili into bowls and serve.

Vegetarian Chili

Makes 8 servings

Ingredients

1 (19 oz.) can black bean soup

1 (15 oz.) can kidney beans, rinsed and drained

1 (15 oz.) can garbanzo beans, rinsed and drained

1 (16 oz.) can vegetarian baked beans

1 (14.5 oz.) can chopped tomatoes, undrained

1 (15 oz.) can whole kernel corn, drained

1 large onion, chopped

1 large green bell pepper, seeded and chopped

2 stalks celery, chopped

2 cloves garlic, minced

1 T. chili powder

1 T. dried parsley

1 T. dried oregano

1 T. dried basil

Directions

Combine the black bean soup, kidney beans, garbanzo beans and baked beans in a 5- to 6-quart slow cooker. Add the tomatoes with liquid, corn, onion, bell pepper, celery and garlic; mix well. Season with chili powder, parsley, oregano and basil. Mix everything together until well combined. Cover the slow cooker and cook on high for at least 2 hours or on low for 4 hours. Ladle the chili into bowls and serve.

Souper Tip

Wine or beer can add wonderful flavor as an addition to soup and stew. Add wine at a ratio of no more than ¼ cup of wine to 1 quart of soup. Add beer at a ratio of 1 cup of beer to 3 cups of soup. About 40% of the alcohol in the wine or beer will remain after 15 minutes of simmering. Only 5% of the alcohol will remain after the soup has simmered for 2½ hours.

Ham and Lentil Soup

Makes 6 servings

Ingredients

1 C. dried lentils, rinsed
1 C. chopped celery
1 C. chopped carrots
1 C. chopped onion
2 cloves garlic, minced
1½ C. cooked diced ham
½ tsp. dried basil

¼ tsp. dried thyme
½ tsp. dried oregano
¼ tsp. pepper
1 bay leaf
4 C. chicken broth
2 T. plus 2 tsp. tomato sauce

Directions

Combine the lentils, celery, carrots, onion, garlic and ham in a 3½- to 6-quart slow cooker. Season with basil, thyme, oregano and pepper. Add the bay leaf and stir gently. Stir in the chicken broth, tomato sauce and 1 cup water. Cover the slow cooker and cook on high for 6 hours or on low for 11 hours. Discard the bay leaf. Ladle the soup into bowls and serve.

Split Pea and Sausage Soup

Makes 8 servings

Ingredients

1 lb. dried split peas
1 lb. smoked sausage, sliced
5 chicken bouillon cubes
1½ C. chopped carrots
1 C. chopped celery

2 potatoes, peeled and chopped
½ tsp. garlic powder
½ tsp. dried oregano
2 bay leaves
1 medium onion, chopped

Directions

Combine the peas, sausage, bouillon cubes, carrots, celery, potatoes, garlic powder, oregano, bay leaves and onion in a 5- to 6-quart slow cooker. Add 10 cups water and mix well. Cover the slow cooker and cook on high for 4 to 5 hours or on low for 10 hours. Discard the bay leaves. Ladle the soup into bowls and serve.

Souper Tip

To remove fat from the surface of soup, refrigerate the cooked soup overnight. The fat will rise and solidify at the top of the soup. The fat may then be removed by breaking it into smaller pieces with a spoon and lifting away. To skim the fat from hot soup, float an ice cube in the soup to help congeal the fat. Lift the fat away with a large spoon.

Chicken Lime Soup

Makes 7 servings, approximately 180 calories per 1-cup serving

Ingredients

1 (14.5 oz.) can diced tomatoes, undrained

1 C. chopped onion

2 T. seeded and chopped chipotle peppers

3 cloves garlic, minced

2 tsp. dried oregano

1 bay leaf

1½ C. cooked, shredded chicken

6 C. chicken broth

½ C. fresh lime juice

Salt and pepper

1 C. shredded Cheddar and Monterey Jack cheese combination

½ C. chopped fresh cilantro

Directions

In a large saucepan or soup pot over medium-high heat, combine the tomatoes with liquid, onion, peppers, garlic, oregano and bay leaf. Cook, stirring occasionally, for 10 minutes. Add the chicken, chicken broth and lime juice. Mix well and bring to a boil. Reduce the heat to medium-low and simmer for 30 minutes. Discard the bay leaf. Season with salt and pepper to taste. Ladle the soup into bowls and top each serving with a sprinkling of shredded cheese and cilantro.

Southwestern Turkey Soup

Makes 8 servings, approximately 185 calories per 1-cup serving

Ingredients

1½ C. cooked, shredded turkey

4 C. vegetable broth

1 (28 oz.) can whole peeled
tomatoes, undrained

1 (4 oz.) can chopped green
chiles, drained

2 roma tomatoes, seeded
and chopped

1 onion, chopped

2 cloves garlic, crushed

1 T. fresh lime juice

½ tsp. cayenne pepper

½ tsp. ground cumin

Salt and pepper

1 avocado, peeled, pitted
and diced

½ tsp. dried cilantro

1 C. shredded Monterey
Jack cheese

Directions

In a large saucepan or soup pot over medium heat, combine the turkey, vegetable broth, tomatoes with liquid, chiles, roma tomatoes, onion, garlic and lime juice. Season with cayenne, cumin, salt and pepper. Bring to a boil, then reduce the heat to medium-low and simmer for 15 to 20 minutes. Stir in the avocado and cilantro. Continue to simmer for an additional 15 to 20 minutes, until the soup has slightly thickened. Ladle the soup into bowls and garnish each serving with a sprinkling of shredded cheese.

Souper Tip

If soup is boiled for too long, it will begin to lose its color.

Italian Wedding Soup

Makes 6 servings, approximately 190 calories per 1-cup serving

Ingredients

½ lb. extra-lean ground beef

1 egg, lightly beaten

2 T. Italian-seasoned bread crumbs

1 T. grated Parmesan cheese

2 T. chopped fresh basil

1 T. chopped fresh parsley

2 green onions, sliced

5¾ C. chicken broth

2 C. finely sliced escarole or spinach

Zest of 1 lemon

½ C. uncooked orzo

Additional Parmesan cheese, optional

Directions

In a medium bowl, combine the ground beef, egg, bread crumbs, 1 tablespoon Parmesan cheese, basil, parsley and green onions. Mix well until all the ingredients are evenly combined. Shape into ¾″ meatballs; set aside. Heat the chicken broth in a large saucepan or soup pot over high heat; bring to a boil. Drop the meatballs into the boiling broth. Stir in the escarole, lemon zest and orzo. Return to a boil, then reduce the heat to medium. Keep at a rolling boil for 10 minutes or until the orzo is tender, stirring often. Ladle the soup into bowls and top each serving with a sprinkling of additional grated Parmesan cheese, if desired.

Manhattan-Style Clam Chowder

Makes 4 servings, approximately 165 calories per 1-cup serving

Ingredients

4 oz. Canadian bacon, diced

1 large Spanish onion, chopped

1 stalk celery, thinly sliced

1 (10 oz.) can clam juice

1 (15 oz.) can whole chopped tomatoes, undrained

2 medium red potatoes, chopped

2 bay leaves

¼ tsp. lemon pepper

1 (6 oz.) can minced clams, undrained

Salt and pepper

¼ C. chopped fresh parsley

Directions

Sauté the diced Canadian bacon in a large saucepan or soup pot over medium-high heat. Add the onion and celery and continue to sauté until the onion is transparent, about 3 minutes. Stir in the clam juice, tomatoes with liquid, potatoes, bay leaves and lemon pepper. Cover the saucepan and bring to a boil. Reduce the heat and simmer, uncovered, until the potatoes are tender, about 12 to 15 minutes. Stir in the clams with liquid and simmer for 5 minutes. Season with salt and pepper to taste. Discard the bay leaves. Ladle the soup into bowls and top each serving with a sprinkling of parsley.

Wild Rice and Three-Mushroom Soup

Makes 6 servings, approximately 190 calories per 1-cup serving

Ingredients

1 oz. dried porcini mushrooms

1 oz. dried shiitake mushrooms

3 T. unsalted butter, divided

1 (8 oz.) pkg. sliced white mushrooms

4 large shallots, chopped

2 large carrots, peeled and chopped

1 stalk celery, chopped

½ C. uncooked wild rice

4 C. vegetable broth

¼ C. chopped fresh parsley

¼ C. dry sherry

Salt and pepper

Directions

In a microwave, bring 2 cups of water to a boil in a glass bowl or measuring cup. Add the porcini and shiitake mushrooms to the boiling water and let soak at least 20 minutes. Meanwhile, melt 1 tablespoon butter in a large saucepan or soup pot over medium-high heat. Add the sliced white mushrooms and sauté until tender. Transfer the sautéed mushrooms to a plate; set aside. Add the remaining 2 tablespoons butter to the saucepan. Add the shallots and sauté until softened, about 3 minutes. Add the carrots and celery and continue to cook until softened, about 4 minutes. Stir in the wild rice and vegetable broth. Bring to a boil over medium-high heat. Meanwhile, strain the liquid from the soaking mushrooms through a fine-hole sieve into the soup pot. Place the mushrooms on a cutting board. Remove any tough stems and slice the caps into ¼″ wide strips; add to the soup. Bring the soup to a simmer, partially covered, over medium-low heat for 30 minutes, or until the rice is tender. Add the sautéed white mushrooms along with any liquid from the plate. Stir in the parsley and sherry. Season with salt and pepper to taste. Ladle the soup into bowls and serve.

Chipotle Tomato Soup

Makes 5 servings, approximately 140 calories per 1-cup serving

Ingredients

2 T. olive oil

1 C. chopped onion

2 (14.5 oz.) cans diced
tomatoes, undrained

2 medium carrots, chopped

1 (14 oz.) can low-sodium
chicken broth

¼ C. light Thousand Island
reduced-fat dressing

1 T. seeded and chopped
chipotle pepper in adobo
sauce

Directions

Heat the olive oil in a large saucepan or deep skillet over medium-high heat. Add the onion and sauté until tender. Stir in the tomatoes with liquid, carrots and chicken broth; mix well. Bring to a boil, then reduce the heat to medium-low and simmer for 15 minutes, or until the vegetables are tender, stirring occasionally. Transfer the hot soup to a blender or food processor, working in batches. Process until smooth. Blend the Thousand Island dressing and chipotle pepper with adobo sauce with the last batch of soup. Return all the soup to the saucepan and cook until heated through. Ladle the soup into bowls and serve. Serve warm or chilled.

Cream-Free Creamy Broccoli Soup

Makes 8 servings, approximately 160 calories per 1-cup serving

Ingredients

3 T. vegetable oil

2 medium carrots, chopped

2 stalks celery, chopped

1 medium onion, chopped

2 (14 oz.) cans fat-free, reduced-sodium chicken broth

½ tsp. pepper

2 small bunches broccoli, chopped

½ C. uncooked instant white rice

2 C. milk

¼ C. grated Parmesan cheese

Directions

Heat the vegetable oil in a large saucepan or soup pot over medium-high heat. Add the carrots, celery and onion; sauté until tender, about 5 minutes. Stir in the chicken broth and pepper. Bring to a boil. Stir in the broccoli and rice. Reduce the heat to medium-low and simmer for 10 to 15 minutes, or until the vegetables are tender, stirring frequently. Transfer the hot soup to a blender or food processor, working in batches. Process until smooth. Return the soup to the saucepan and add the milk and Parmesan cheese. Continue to cook until heated through. Ladle the soup into bowls and serve.

Zucchini Soup Margherita

Makes 4 servings, approximately 105 calories per 1-cup serving

Ingredients

2 tsp. olive oil

1 small zucchini, halved
lengthwise and sliced

1 medium onion, chopped

4 cloves garlic, minced

3½ C. chicken broth

2 to 3 roma tomatoes, sliced

1 tsp. balsamic vinegar

Salt and pepper

½ C. shredded part-skim
mozzarella cheese

½ C. chopped fresh basil

Directions

Heat the olive oil in a large saucepan or soup pot over medium-high heat. Add the zucchini, onion and garlic; sauté for 3 to 5 minutes, or until the vegetables begin to brown. Stir in the chicken broth, tomatoes and vinegar. Mix well and season lightly with salt and pepper to taste. Cover the saucepan and bring to a boil. Reduce the heat to medium and simmer for 10 minutes. Ladle the soup into bowls and garnish each serving with 2 tablespoons shredded mozzarella cheese and 2 tablespoons chopped basil.

Souper Tip

For an easy-to-make bread bowl, purchase a 1-pound loaf of frozen bread dough; thaw in the refrigerator overnight. Once thawed, cut the dough into fourths, and shape each section into a circular dome. Place the domes on a baking sheet, cover and let rise for 4 to 7 hours. Preheat the oven to 350°. Bake the dough for 20 to 25 minutes or until golden brown. Let cool before cutting the top ¼ off the bread. Scoop out some of the bread inside and fill the bowl with soup.

Index

Collect all 4 Titles in the

super bowl

Series

the
super bowl
50 Sensational Salads

the
super bowl
50 Delicious Dips

the
super bowl
50 Pleasing Pastas

from  Products